A TRUE BOОК

CIRCULATORY SYSTEM

Alicia Green

Children's Press®
An imprint of Scholastic Inc.

Content Consultant
Tom Johnson
Former Director, Respiratory Care, Long Island University
Professor of Cardiopulmonary Medicine

Copyright © 2024 by Scholastic Inc.

All rights reserved. Published by Children's Press, an imprint of Scholastic Inc., *Publishers since 1920.*
SCHOLASTIC, CHILDREN'S PRESS, A TRUE BOOK™, and associated logos are trademarks and/or registered trademarks of Scholastic Inc.

The publisher does not have any control over and does not assume any responsibility for author or third-party websites or their content.

No part of this publication may be reproduced, stored in a retrieval system, or transmitted in any form or by any means, electronic, mechanical, photocopying, recording, or otherwise, without written permission of the publisher. For information regarding permission, write to Scholastic Inc., Attention: Permissions Department, 557 Broadway, New York, NY 10012.

Library of Congress Cataloging-in-Publication Data available
ISBN 978-1-339-02093-8 (library binding) | ISBN 978-1-339-02094-5 (paperback)

10 9 8 7 6 5 4 3 2 1   24 25 26 27 28

Printed in China 62
First edition, 2024

Design by Kathleen Petelinsek
Series produced by Spooky Cheetah Press

Find the Truth!

Everything you are about to read is true *except* for one of the sentences on this page.

Which one is **TRUE**?

T or F There are four main blood types.

T or F The vena cava is the largest artery in your body.

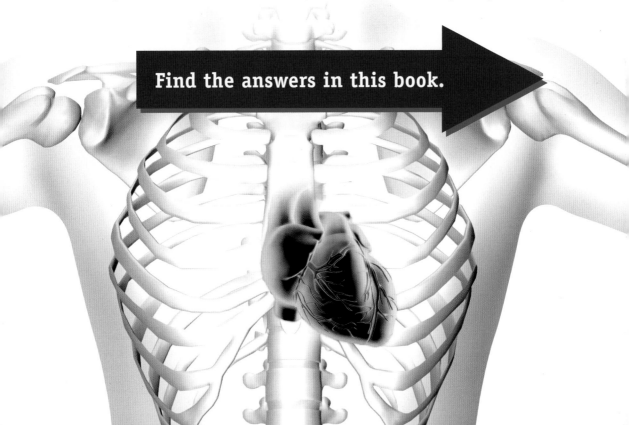

Find the answers in this book.

What's in This Book?

Red blood cells
are flexible, so
they can move
through your
body easily.

4

The BIG Truth

A blood pressure test is one way to determine the health of your circulatory system.

Teamwork!

How does the circulatory system interact with your body's other systems? **30**

4 Problems with the Circulatory System

What illnesses can affect the circulatory system, and how are they treated? **33**

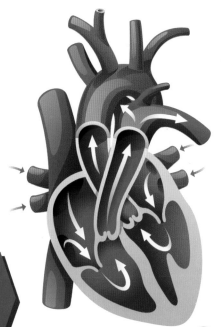

Your heart has four hollow spaces called chambers. Blood flows through them.

5

Each day, the blood in your body travels about 12,000 miles (19,000 kilometers). That's five times the distance from one coast of the United States to the other.

INTRODUCTION

Have you ever been running or playing and noticed that your **heart is beating faster** than usual? That is your **circulatory system** working to keep you moving. Your circulatory system is the group of **organs** that **pump blood** throughout your body, **carrying oxygen**, **nutrients**, and **hormones** to your **cells**. The circulatory system also **removes waste** from your cells and **protects you** from disease.

    Your circulatory system has **three main parts**: **the heart**, **blood vessels**, and **blood**. Each part has an important function, and they all **work together** as a team. Read on to learn more!

Exercise is one key to a healthy heart.

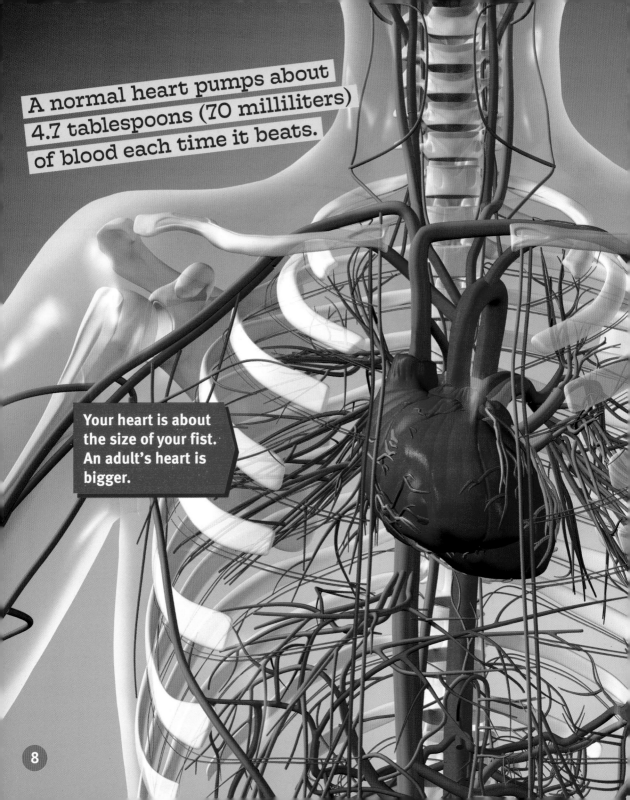

A normal heart pumps about 4.7 tablespoons (70 milliliters) of blood each time it beats.

Your heart is about the size of your fist. An adult's heart is bigger.

The Power Station

Your heart is the most important organ in your circulatory system. It's located near the center of your chest, on the left side, between your lungs. The heart is a muscle that contracts (squeezes) and relaxes in a constant rhythm. That is how your heart pumps blood through your body. The heart is made of different parts that work together to keep your blood moving.

2 + 2 = 4

The heart has four hollow spaces called chambers. The two upper chambers are the right atrium and left atrium. The lower chambers are the right ventricle and left ventricle. Blood from your body flows into the right atrium and then into the right ventricle. From there, it goes to your lungs. Blood from your lungs enters the left atrium and then moves into the left ventricle. From there, it is pumped out to your body.

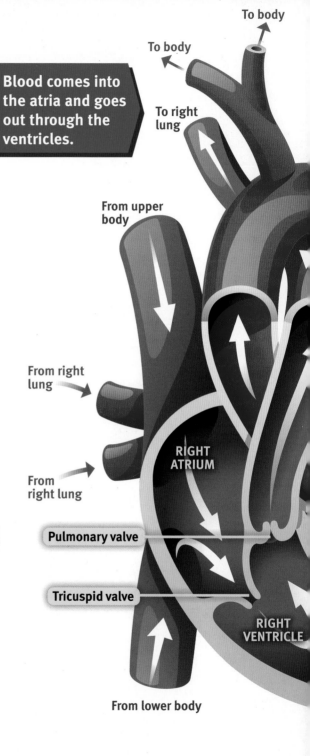

Blood comes into the atria and goes out through the ventricles.

To body

To body

To right lung

From upper body

From right lung

From right lung

RIGHT ATRIUM

Pulmonary valve

Tricuspid valve

RIGHT VENTRICLE

From lower body

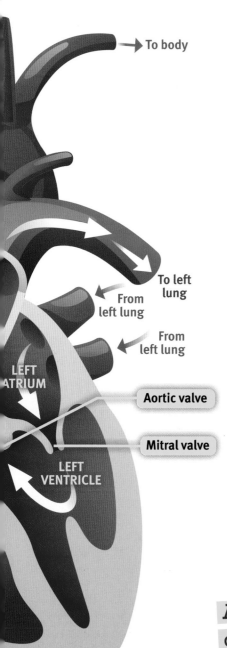

To body

To body

To left lung

From left lung

From left lung

LEFT ATRIUM

Aortic valve

Mitral valve

LEFT VENTRICLE

The Doors to Your Heart

The heart chambers have four valves that are made of strong, thin flaps of tissue. The valves act like doors and are responsible for keeping your blood moving in only one direction. A valve opens to let blood pass through and then quickly closes so that it cannot flow backward. The opening and closing of our heart valves is what creates the *lub, dub, lub, dub* sound that is our heartbeat.

Adults have a resting heart rate of 60 to 100 beats per minute.

Going Around in Circles

A single heartbeat—that contracting and relaxing that you read about—goes through a two-part cycle. The part of the **cardiac** cycle when your heart muscle relaxes is known as the diastole [dye-AS-tuh-lee] stage. During this stage, your heart chambers fill with blood. The systole [SIS-tuh-lee] stage is when your heart muscle contracts. That is when blood is pumped to the lungs and other parts of your body.

One cardiac cycle usually takes less than a second.

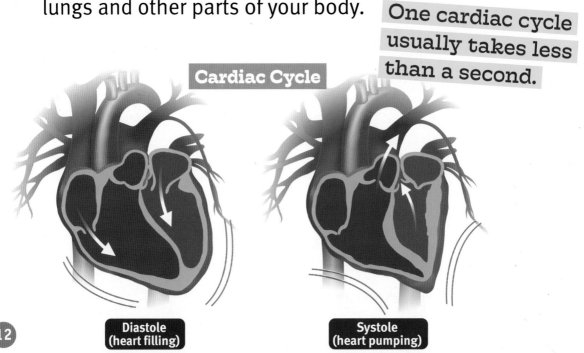

Cardiac Cycle

Diastole
(heart filling)

Systole
(heart pumping)

Are You Stressed?

Our hearts do not always pump at the same speed. At rest, most kids' hearts beat between 75 and 118 times per minute. Our heart rate speeds up when we exercise, but also when we are scared, nervous, or very excited. Being scared, nervous, or excited is called being under stress. In these situations, a hormone called adrenaline [uh-DREN-uh-lin] is released into our bodies to make us ready for whatever comes next. That hormone causes our heart rate and breathing to temporarily speed up.

Stress isn't always bad.

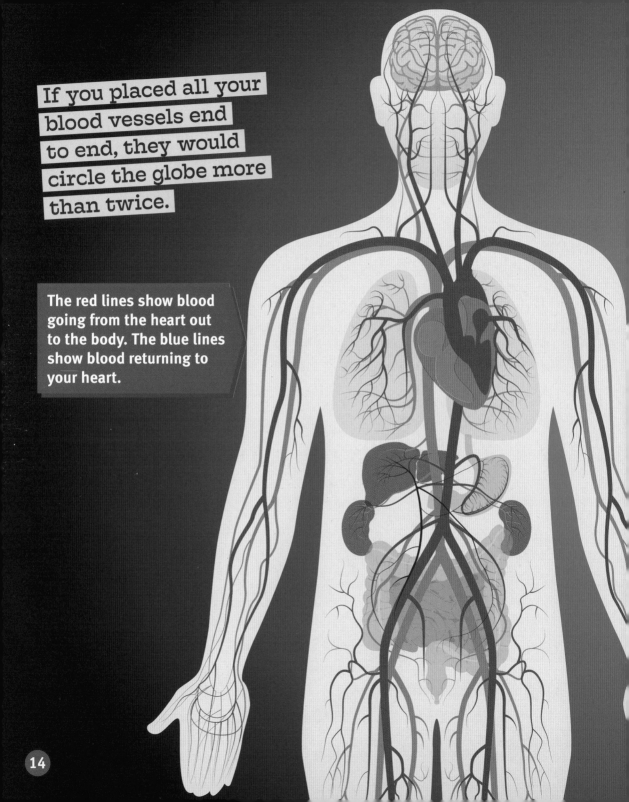

If you placed all your blood vessels end to end, they would circle the globe more than twice.

The red lines show blood going from the heart out to the body. The blue lines show blood returning to your heart.

A Super Roadway System

Blood vessels are like roads. They are the tubes that blood travels through to move throughout your body. They are partly made of muscle. There are three types of blood vessels: arteries, capillaries, and veins. These blood vessels are divided into two specific pathways: the **pulmonary** circuit and the **systemic** circuit. The pulmonary circuit circulates blood between the heart and the lungs. The systemic circuit carries blood between the heart and the rest of the body.

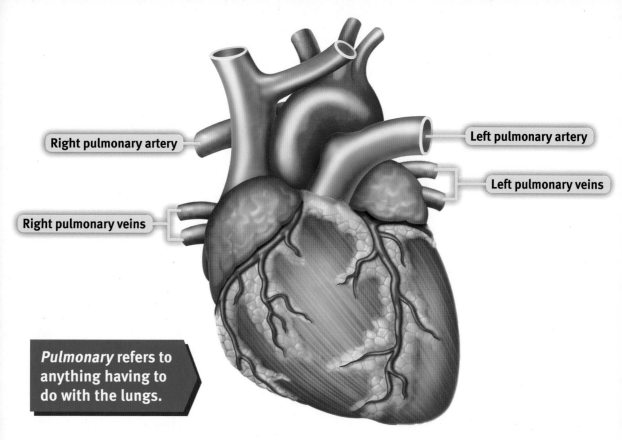

Right pulmonary artery

Left pulmonary artery

Left pulmonary veins

Right pulmonary veins

Pulmonary refers to anything having to do with the lungs.

The Pulmonary Circuit

Your heart's pulmonary arteries connect to your right and left lungs. Pulmonary arteries carry oxygen-poor blood from your heart to your lungs. That is their only job. When the blood gets to your lungs, it becomes oxygenated, and excess carbon dioxide is removed. Then pulmonary veins take the oxygenated blood to your heart.

The Systemic Circuit

In the systemic circuit, arteries are the blood vessels that move oxygen-rich blood away from the heart and around the body. Your heart pumps this blood into the biggest artery in your body—the aorta. The aorta is shaped like a cane. It begins at your heart's left ventricle and passes through your chest and into your **abdomen**.

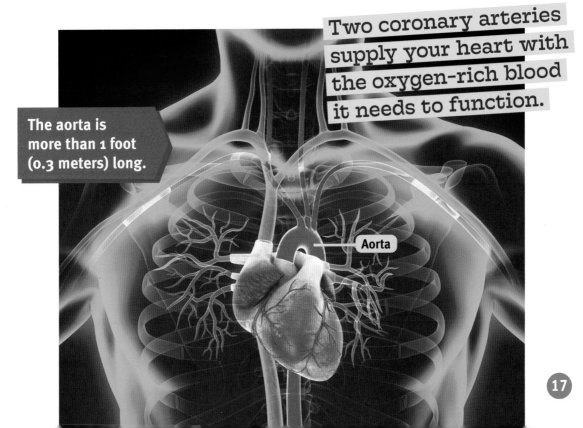

Two coronary arteries supply your heart with the oxygen-rich blood it needs to function.

The aorta is more than 1 foot (0.3 meters) long.

Aorta

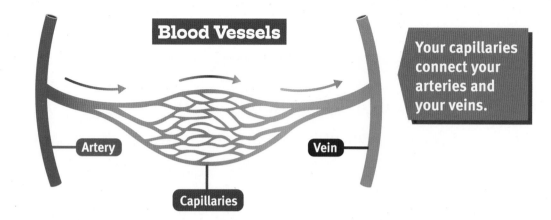

Blood Vessels

Your capillaries connect your arteries and your veins.

Artery

Vein

Capillaries

Making a Connection

Capillaries are the smallest blood vessels. They connect the smallest branches of your arteries to your smallest veins. Oxygen and nutrients pass through the thin walls of your capillaries into the cells. Waste from your cells passes into the capillaries. Then that blood moves from your capillaries into your veins and back to your heart. The nearer your veins get to your heart, the bigger they get. The vena cava is the largest vein in the body.

Our veins have valves to keep the blood moving only in one direction.

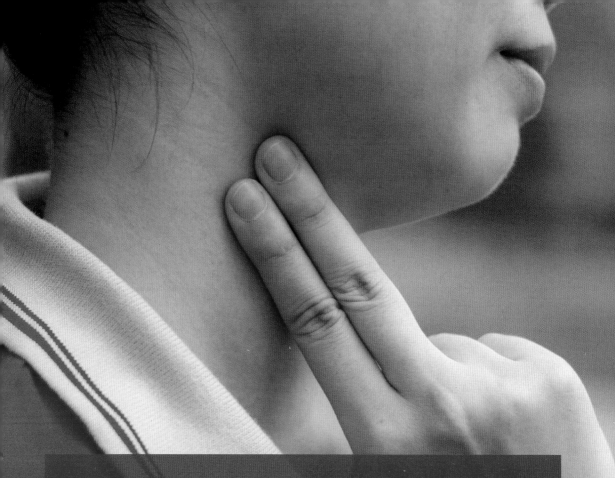

Find Your Beat

Your pulse is a steady beat or throb that is caused by the pressure in your arteries increasing as your heart pumps out blood. It indicates the number of times your heart beats in a minute. There are many places in the body where a person can feel their pulse. It's usually in a spot where an artery passes close to the skin. The easiest spots to feel a pulse are at the wrist on your thumb side, either side of the neck, and the inside of an elbow. You can also feel your pulse behind your knees. Some kids can feel a pulse on the top of their feet too!

It takes one minute for the blood to go around the body.

Bleeding helps clean a wound.

A Vital Body Fluid

If you've ever gotten a cut or a scrape, then you've seen what your blood looks like. But if you could examine your blood under a microscope, it would look a lot different. You might be surprised to see that your blood is made up of different parts. The liquid part is called plasma. The solid parts are red and white blood cells and platelets. Almost all of these solid components are produced by your bone marrow. That is the soft, spongy material that is found in the center of your bones.

Plasma is mostly made up of water.

Plasma is a clear yellow fluid.

Transporting Nutrients

The majority of your blood—55 percent—is plasma. It brings nutrients and hormones to your body's cells and carries away waste. It keeps your blood vessels from collapsing too.

Plasma also carries your blood cells throughout your body. If you were looking at plasma under a microscope, you'd see your red and white blood cells and platelets floating in it.

Oxygen Delivery

Red blood cells are shaped like flattened disks and are flexible. They transport oxygen from your lungs to your body's cells. Each red blood cell contains hemoglobin, which is the protein that carries oxygen. Oxygen in your hemoglobin is what gives your blood its bright red color. Your red blood cells also carry carbon dioxide waste to your lungs, where it is breathed out.

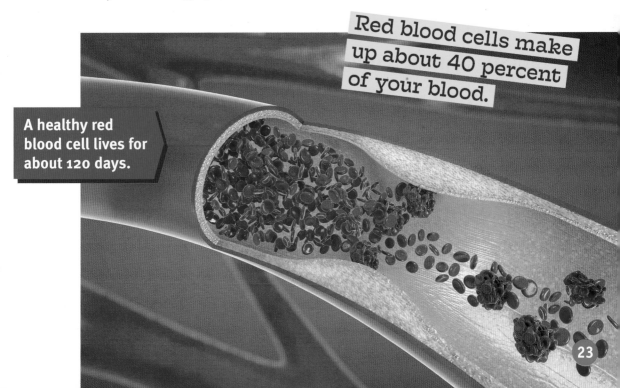

Red blood cells make up about 40 percent of your blood.

A healthy red blood cell lives for about 120 days.

Your Body's Protectors

White blood cells protect your body from disease. These tiny cells travel through your bloodstream to fight off viruses, bacteria, and other unknown invaders. When specific white blood cells locate a part of your body that is under attack, they signal for more white blood cells to help defend it. They fight off attackers by producing **antibodies**. These proteins in your blood attach to the invader. They help other specialized types of white blood cells identify the invader and destroy it. Some white blood cells change their shape so they can wrap themselves around an invader and gobble it up.

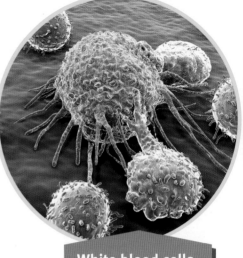

White blood cells fight an invader (shown in yellow).

White blood cells make up just 1 percent of your blood. But they multiply rapidly to fight infection.

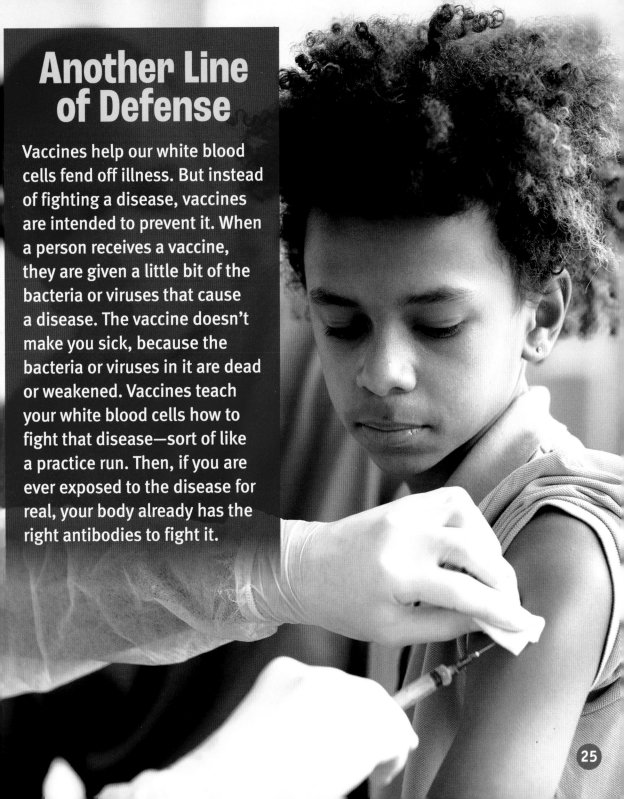

Another Line of Defense

Vaccines help our white blood cells fend off illness. But instead of fighting a disease, vaccines are intended to prevent it. When a person receives a vaccine, they are given a little bit of the bacteria or viruses that cause a disease. The vaccine doesn't make you sick, because the bacteria or viruses in it are dead or weakened. Vaccines teach your white blood cells how to fight that disease—sort of like a practice run. Then, if you are ever exposed to the disease for real, your body already has the right antibodies to fight it.

Stop the Bleeding

If we get a cut or a scrape, platelets are the blood cells that make the bleeding stop. When a blood vessel breaks, it sends a signal. Platelets respond to this signal and arrive at the injured area. The platelets then come together to form a clot—which is when your blood thickens. The clot acts like a plug and stops the bleeding.

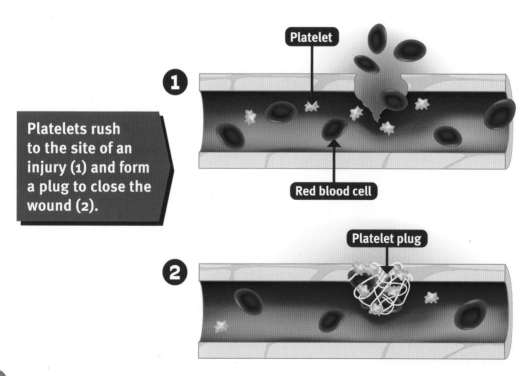

Platelets rush to the site of an injury (1) and form a plug to close the wound (2).

Platelet

❶

Red blood cell

Platelet plug

❷

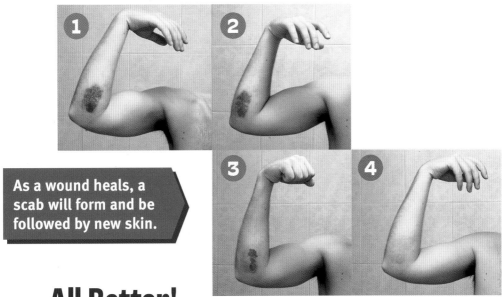

As a wound heals, a scab will form and be followed by new skin.

All Better!

All the elements of your blood work together to treat a wound. After platelets stop the bleeding, white blood cells help clear the area of germs and begin repairing the cells. Red blood cells help the area heal and grow new blood vessels. If the wound was on the skin, little by little, the plug created by the platelets turns into a scab that protects the wound. It will usually take four to six weeks for a wound to heal. During that time, the wound should be kept clean and covered with antibiotic cream and a bandage.

It Takes All Types

All humans have a blood type, which is determined by the presence or absence of **antigens** on their red blood cells. There are four main blood types: A, B, AB, and O. And they can be negative or positive. If a person's blood type is positive, that means their red blood cells have a protein on their surface called Rhesus (Rh) factor. A person with a negative blood type doesn't have this protein.

Timeline: Circulatory Medicine History

1628
Dr. William Harvey publishes his thesis that the heart pumps blood throughout the body.

1665
Dr. Richard Lower performs the first successful blood transfusion between dogs.

1695
Antonie van Leeuwenhoek first describes red blood cells.

1842
Physician Alfred Donné identifies platelets. The following year, Gabriel Andral and William Addison describe white blood cells.

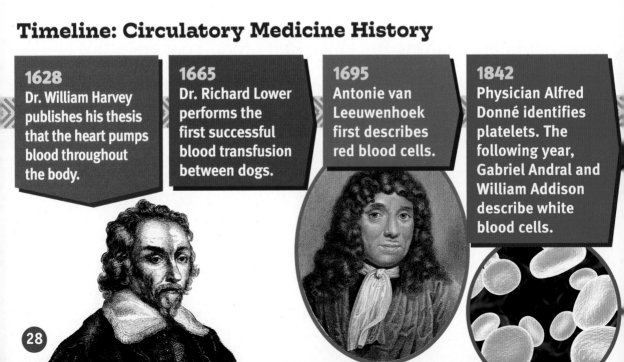

Some for Me, Some for You

A blood transfusion is when blood is taken from one person and given to another. Some people require blood transfusions if they are injured, have surgery, or have diseases that affect their blood. When a person receives a blood transfusion, a narrow tube is placed in a vein in their arm so the blood can be delivered to the circulatory system.

A blood transfusion is needed every two seconds in the United States.

1900
Physician Karl Landsteiner identifies the first three blood types: A, B, and C (later changed to O).

1938
Dr. Charles Drew improves the blood donation process. Thanks to him, blood to be used in transfusions can be stored for longer periods of time.

1967
Dr. Christiaan Barnard performs the first successful heart transplant.

2022
Scientists create a wearable ultrasound device that assesses how a patient's heart is functioning.

Teamwork!

The circulatory system does not function on its own. Find out how it works with other systems in your body to keep you running!

Respiratory System:

Your lungs provide the oxygen that is carried to all parts of the body by the circulatory system. Your respiratory system is also responsible for removing the carbon dioxide and water from your blood that cells produce as waste products.

Nervous System:

Your circulatory system provides the oxygen-rich blood your brain needs to survive. In turn, your nervous system controls how quickly or slowly your heart beats.

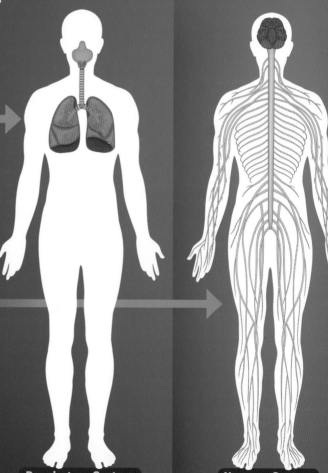

Respiratory System

Nervous System

Digestive System:

Your circulatory system carries oxygen and nutrients to the organs in your digestive system, which include your mouth, stomach, and intestines. Nutrients from the food you eat are transferred from the small intestine into your bloodstream to be carried to the rest of your body.

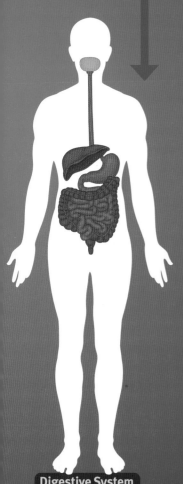

Digestive System

Muscular System:

Your heart is a powerful muscle. There are also muscles in your blood vessels that help move your blood along. There are hundreds of other muscles in your body, as well, and they all need the oxygen supplied by the circulatory system in order to function.

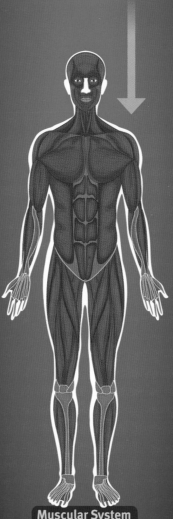

Muscular System

Skeletal System:

The circulatory system nourishes your skeletal system with oxygen-rich blood. Part of your skeletal system's job is to produce some of the components of your blood—your body's blood cells and platelets. That happens inside your bones, in your bone marrow.

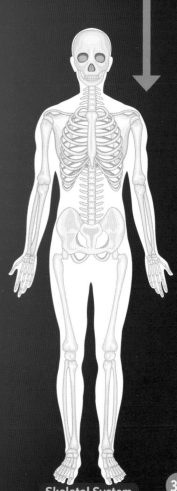

Skeletal System

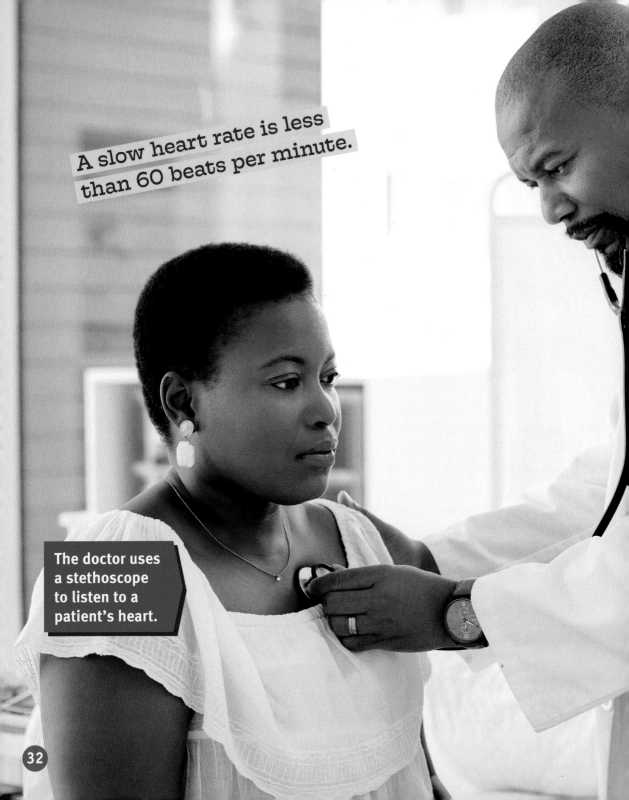

A slow heart rate is less than 60 beats per minute.

The doctor uses a stethoscope to listen to a patient's heart.

Problems with the Circulatory System

Sometimes our circulatory system doesn't work the way it should. When one part of this system gets sick and can't do its job, your whole body feels the impact. An irregular heartbeat is called an arrhythmia [ay-RITH-me-uh]. It is one fairly common disorder. That is when your heart beats too fast, too slow, or in an irregular rhythm. Keep reading to learn about other illnesses that affect the circulatory system and how they are treated.

Understanding Anemia

Anemia is a condition that happens when a person doesn't have enough red blood cells. As a result, not enough oxygen gets to a person's different body systems, so they can't function properly. A person who is anemic may look pale and feel dizzy. Usually, kids who become anemic lack iron, which is a nutrient that helps make hemoglobin. Iron can be found in foods such as meat, eggs, and leafy green vegetables.

A person who is anemic is often cold and tired.

Kids should have 4 million to 5.5 million red blood cells per microliter of blood.

A Different Type of Anemia

Sickle cell anemia is different from the anemia you just read about. It is not caused by a nutritional deficiency, and it cannot be cured. Sickle cell anemia is a disorder that is passed down from parents to their child. It causes many red blood cells to take on a crescent moon shape. Red blood cells have to be flexible to move through arteries, capillaries, and veins. Sickle cells are not flexible, so they cannot move around the body easily. That means less oxygen gets carried to different parts of the body. These cells also get stuck in blood vessels, blocking the flow of blood and causing pain, especially in the chest.

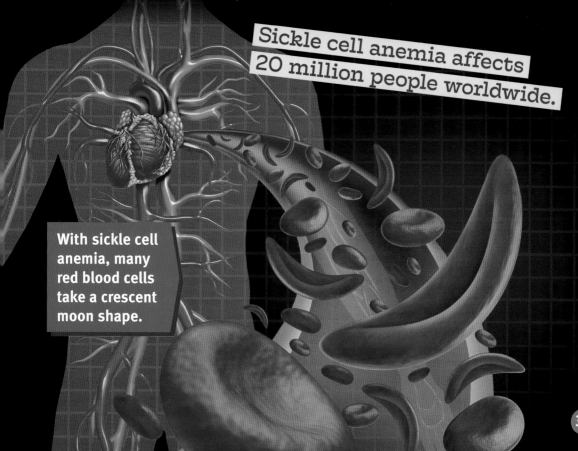

Sickle cell anemia affects 20 million people worldwide.

With sickle cell anemia, many red blood cells take a crescent moon shape.

A heart attack occurs about every 40 seconds in the United States.

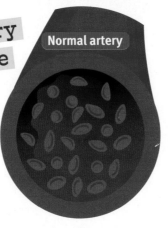

Normal artery

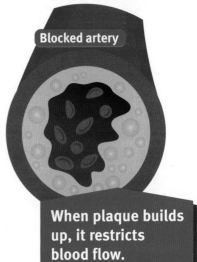

Blocked artery

When plaque builds up, it restricts blood flow.

What Is a Heart Attack?

Heart attacks happen when coronary arteries that supply blood to the heart become too narrow and blocked. They may also become less flexible. That is caused by a buildup of **cholesterol**, fats, and other substances that are known as plaque. When the arteries are blocked, less blood—and therefore less oxygen—can get to the heart. People with a history of heart disease visit their doctor often to check for narrowing of these arteries. If an artery is blocked, the doctor can pass a tiny balloon into the artery to widen it. A tiny tube, called a stent, may also be placed in the artery to keep it open.

What Is a Stroke?

Strokes restrict or reduce blood flow to brain cells, which will begin to die within minutes. A hemorrhagic [hem-uh-RAJ-ik] stroke occurs when an artery in the brain bursts. In an ischemic [i-SKEE-mik] stroke, blood flow from an artery is blocked by plaque or a blood clot. People who are at risk for an ischemic stroke, or have had one before, can be treated with medications that thin the blood. Their doctor may also tell them to take aspirin, which will make platelets less likely to form clots.

About 80 percent of strokes could be prevented.

Managing Blood Pressure

Blood pressure is a measure that shows the amount of force the heart is using to pump blood. High blood pressure is called hypertension. That is when the force of the heart contracting or the pressure of the blood pushing against the artery walls is too high. The heart and arteries are working too hard. Regular exercise and a healthy diet are two ways to keep blood pressure low. Many people need medication to manage their blood pressure—even when they follow a healthy lifestyle.

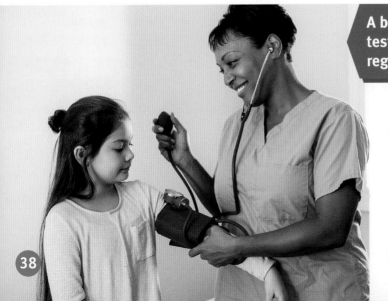

A blood pressure test is part of a regular checkup.

Most Americans with high blood pressure don't know they have it. Often, there are no symptoms.

A healthy circulatory system helps us have fun!

A Complex Body

Think of your body as a city. For this city to work, it needs roads to link to all the important places. Your veins and arteries are the roadways. They allow your blood cells to travel to different parts of your body. Your blood is like a vehicle delivering what your body needs to stay healthy and taking away waste. And your heart is the city's center— it keeps everything moving along!

Circulatory Care

Doctors and nurses work with us to prevent and treat disease. Here are a few health care professionals who treat the circulatory system, and some of the tests they may perform.

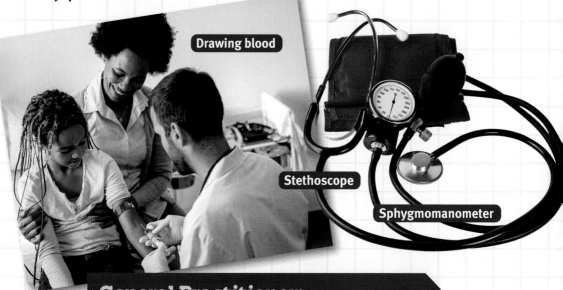

Drawing blood

Stethoscope

Sphygmomanometer

General Practitioner:

This is the doctor a person sees regularly for checkups. General practitioners (GPs) can listen to someone's heartbeat using a stethoscope. They use a sphygmomanometer [sfig-moh-meh-NAH-mi-tuhr] to check blood pressure. A GP or nurse may also draw blood for a blood test.

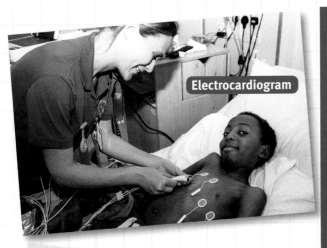
Electrocardiogram

Cardiologist:

A cardiologist specializes in treating heart conditions. Cardiologists conduct electrocardiograms (EKGs), exercise stress tests, and blood tests to determine heart health. EKGs monitor the electrical activity in a person's heart. An exercise stress test shows how the heart functions during different levels of physical activity.

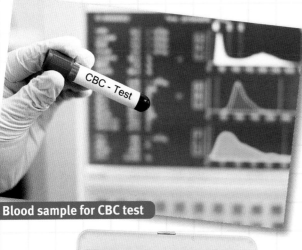
CBC - Test
Blood sample for CBC test

Hematologist:

These doctors specialize in diseases that affect the blood. A hematologist conducts a complete blood count (CBC) test. This test measures and counts a person's red and white blood cells and platelets. Another test is the prothrombin time test. It measures how quickly a blood clot forms.

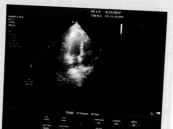
Ultrasound machine

Vascular Doctor:

These doctors treat problems of the blood vessels, specifically arteries and veins. A vascular doctor will take an ultrasound to check blood flow in the blood vessels of someone's arms, neck, and legs. They also test to see how blood flows through the blood vessels and heart.

Protect Your Circulatory System

Keeping your circulatory system healthy is important. And if you take care of it now, you will have a healthier future. Here are four things that you can do to protect your heart health and more.

Eat Healthy

A healthy diet can help keep your arteries clear. Leafy green vegetables and fruits are good food choices. And whole grains help move fats out of your body. Eating right means also avoiding foods that are not good for you. Stay away from deep-fried foods and foods that have a lot of added salt or sugar.

Exercise

Your heart is a muscle and, just like any other muscle, it needs exercise to stay in top shape. Kids should get 60 minutes of physical activity every day. You can walk, ride a bike, or do anything that makes your heart beat faster. These types of exercises help improve your blood flow.

Rest

If you want a healthy heart, you need a good night's sleep. Experts suggest that 6- to 13-year-olds get 9 to 12 hours of sleep daily. Getting the right amount of sleep can reduce your chances of developing heart disease or experiencing a heart attack or stroke later in life.

Do Not Smoke or Vape

Smoking produces carbon monoxide, which takes up the space in red blood cells that should hold oxygen. It also increases the formation of plaque, which narrows and stiffens blood vessels. Chemicals in cigarette smoke cause the blood to thicken and form blood clots.

True Statistics

Average weight of an adult heart: 10 ounces

Average number of times the heart beats every day: 100,000

Average number of times the heart beats in a year: 35 million

Normal heart rate of an adult: 60 to 100 beats per minute

Normal heart rate of kids between 5 and 12 years old: 75 to 118 beats per minute

Distance the body's blood travels daily: 12,000 miles (19,000 kilometers)

Average life span of healthy red blood cells: 120 days

Average number of red blood cells in adults: 25 trillion

Number of days platelets live in the body: 7 to 10

Average number of platelets an adult produces daily: 100 billion

Did you find the truth?

T There are four main blood types.

F The vena cava is the largest artery in your body.

Resources

Other books in this series:

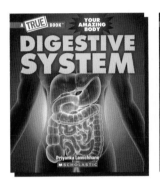 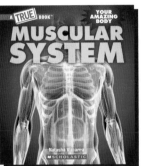  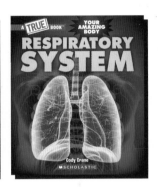

You can also look at:

Corcoran, Mary K. *The Circulatory Story*. Illustrated by Jef Czekaj. Watertown, MA: Charlesbridge, 2010.

Graham, Ian. *The Science of Scabs and Pus: The Sticky Truth about Blood*. New York: Scholastic, 2018.

Hansen, Grace. *Circulatory System*. Minneapolis, MN: Abdo, 2018

Kenney, Karen Latchana. *Circulatory System*. Minneapolis, MN: Pogo, 2019.

Knowledge Encyclopedia Human Body! New York: DK Publishing, 2017.

Glossary

abdomen (AB-duh-muhn) the front part of your body between your chest and hips

antibodies (AN-ti-bah-dees) proteins that your blood makes to stop an infection that has entered your body

antigens (AN-ti-jenz) substances that are foreign to the body and create an immune response

cardiac (KAHR-dee-ak) of or having to do with the heart

cells (SELZ) the smallest units of an animal or a plant

cholesterol (kuh-LES-tuh-rawl) a fatty substance that humans and animals need to digest food and produce certain vitamins and hormones; too much cholesterol in the blood can increase the possibility of heart disease

hormones (HOR-monez) chemical substances made by your body that affect the way your body grows, develops, and functions

organs (OR-guhnz) parts of the body, such as the heart or the kidneys, that have a certain purpose

pulmonary (PUL-muh-ner-ee) of or having to do with the lungs

systemic (sis-TEM-ik) supplying the parts of the body that receive blood from the aorta rather than the pulmonary artery

Index

Page numbers in **bold** indicate illustrations.

About the Author

Alicia Green is a journalist and writer with a passion for storytelling. Her stories reach third- to sixth-grade students across the United States. She enjoys writing articles that intrigue children and teach them something new. Her goal is to help educate kids in fun and unique ways. *Circulatory System* is Alicia's second True Book. Her first book was *What Is Money?*

Photos ©: back cover: andresr/Getty Images; 4: Christoph Burgstedt/Getty Images; 5 top: kali9/Getty Images; 5 bottom: jackom/Getty Images; 6-7: FatCamera/Getty Images; 8-9: artpartner-images/Getty Images; 10-11: jackom/Getty Images; 12: Graphic_BKK1979/Getty Images; 13: andresr/Getty Images; 17: Nerthuz/Getty Images; 23: Christoph Burgstedt/Getty Images; 24: Juan Gartner/Getty Images; 28 left: The Art Archive/Shutterstock; 28 center: Historia/Shutterstock; 29 left: Everett/Shutterstock; 29 center: Howard University/Moorland-Spingarn Research Center/Charles R. Drew Papers/NLM; 29 right: Xu Laboratory at UC San Diego/Flickr; 32-33: PeopleImages/Getty Images; 34: Zinkevych/Getty Images; 36: art4stock/Getty Images; 37: Jon Feingersh Photography Inc/Getty Images; 38: kali9/Getty Images; 39: SolStock/Getty Images; 40-41 background: billnoll/Getty Images; 41 top: LIFE IN VIEW/Science Source; 41 center: jaruno11/Getty Images; 43 center: Jamie Grill/JGI/Blend Images/Getty Images.

All other photos © Shutterstock.